Oxford United Quiz Book

101 Questions To Test Your Knowledge
Of This Friendly Football Club

Published by Glowworm Press
7 Nuffield Way
Abingdon OX14 1RL

By Chris Carpenter

Oxford United

This book contains one hundred and one informative and entertaining trivia questions, all with multiple choice answers. You will find some questions easy, and some challenging and this book will test your knowledge and memory of the club's long history.

You will be asked a wide range of topics for you to test yourself; questions about players, managers, legends, transfer deals, opponents, fixtures and terrace songs amongst other things thereby guaranteeing you hours of fun and an educational experience. This Oxford United Quiz Book is entertaining and enjoyable for Yellows fans of all ages, testing your understanding of **Oxford United Football Club**.

2019/20 Season Edition

FOREWORD

When I was asked to write a foreword to this book I was flattered.

I have known Chris the author for many years and his knowledge of facts and figures and football in general is phenomenal.

His love for the game and his talent for writing quiz books make him the ideal man to pay homage to my true love Oxford United Football Club.

This book came about as a result of a challenge in a pub!

I do hope you enjoy the book.

Anthony Dillard

Let's start with some relatively easy questions.

1. When were Oxford United founded?
   A. 1873
   B. 1883
   C. 1893

2. What is Oxford United's nickname?
   A. The Blues
   B. The Greens
   C. The Yellows

3. Where does Oxford United play their home games?
   A. Hassam Stadium
   B. Kassam Stadium
   C. Wassam Stadium

4. What is the stadium capacity?
   A. 10,500
   B. 11,500
   C. 12,500

5. Who or what is the club mascot?
   A. Peter the Poacher
   B. Olly The Ox
   C. Ryan Red Nose

6. Who has made the most appearances for the club in total?
   A. Ron Atkinson
   B. Gary Briggs
   C. John Shuker

7. Who has made the most *Football League* appearances for the club?
   A. Ron Atkinson
   B. Cyril Beavon
   C. John Shuker

8. Who is the club's all time record goal scorer in all competitions?
   A. Graham Atkinson
   B. John Constable
   C. Tony Jones

9. Who is the club's record League goal scorer?
   A. John Aldridge
   B. Graham Atkinson
   C. John Constable

10. Which of these is a well known pub near the ground?
    A. The Golden Ball
    B. The Golden Cross
    C. The Golden Eagle

OK, so here are the answers to the first ten questions. If you get eight or more right, you are doing very well so far, but don't get too cocky, as the questions do get harder.

A1. Founded as Headington United in 1893, Oxford United adopted their current name in 1960.

A2. Oxford United's official nickname is The Yellows.

A3. Oxford United plays their home games at the Kassam Stadium.

A4. The Kassam Stadium is an all-seater venue with a current capacity of 12,500.

A5. Olly the Ox is the official club mascot. Give yourself a bonus point if you know there is also a female mascot called Olivia.

A6. Ron Atkinson takes the honour for most appearances for the club, with 559 appearances in total, between 1959 and 1971. He played as a defensive midfielder, what used to be called a "wing-back" and was nicknamed "The Tank".

A7. Although Ron Atkinson played 559 times for the club, quite a few of these games were in non League matches, in the Southern League. John Shuker takes the honour for most appearances in the Football League, with a total of 478 appearances from 1962 to 1977.

A8. Graham Atkinson scored a grand total of 107 goals for the club, in 398 appearances during his time at the club from 1959 to 1974.

A9. It's that man Graham Atkinson again. He scored a total of 97 League goals in his time at the club. Legend.

A10. The area around the ground is not well served by pubs, so most people tend to drink at the stadium. However, if you want a traditional pub, The Golden Ball in Littlemore is the place to go. It is about three quarters of a mile from the ground, so leave plenty of time to get there before kick-off.

OK, now we move onto some questions about the club's records.

11. What is the club's record win in the League?
    A. 7-0
    B. 8-0
    C. 9-0

12. Who did they beat?
    A. Barrow
    B. Crewe Alexandra
    C. Workington

13. In which season?
    A. 1964/65
    B. 1974/75
    C. 1984/85

14. What is the club's record defeat?
    A. 0-7
    B. 0-8
    C. 0-9

15. Who against?
    A. Middlesbrough
    B. Newcastle United
    C. Sunderland

16. In which season?
    A. 1992/93
    B. 1995/96
    C. 1998/99

17. What is the highest number of goals that Oxford United has scored in a League season?
    A. 91
    B. 93
    C. 95

18.   What is the fewest number of goals that Oxford United has conceded in a League season?
    A. 36
    B. 37
    C. 38

19. What is the highest attendance Oxford United has played in front of?
    A. 89,639
    B. 90,396
    C. 91,963

20.   Which of these has made the most appearances as goalkeeper for the club?
    A. Roy Burton
    B. Ryan Clarke
    C. Phil Whitehead

Here are the answers to the last block of questions.

A11. Oxford United's record win is in the League is 7-0. The club's record win in any competition is 9-0, against Wisbech Town in the Southern League back in December 1960.

A12. They beat Barrow 7-0 to record their best ever League victory.

A13. The date for Oxford United's record win was on the 19th December 1964 in the old Division Four (level 4), hence the 1964/65 season.

A14. Oxford United's record defeat is incredibly 0-7.

A15. Oxford United's record defeat was by Sunderland.

A16. The club's record defeat was in League Division One (level 2) back in September 1998, so in the 1998/99 season.

A17. The highest number of League goals scored was 91 in 46 matches in Division Three (level 3) in the 1983/84 season.

A18. Proving that Oxford were a good side in the mid 1980s, the fewest number of goals conceded in a season was 36 in 42 matches in Division Two (level 2) in the 1984/85 season.

A19. 90,396 people watched the League Cup Final between Oxford United and QPR at Wembley Stadium on 20th April 1986.

A20. Goalkeeper Roy Burton made a grand total of 447 appearances for the club from 1971 to 1982.

Here is the next set of questions.

21. How many seasons have Oxford United played in the top tier of English football?
    A. 1
    B. 2
    C. 3

22. What is the club's highest ever finish in the League?
    A. 18th in Division One
    B. 4th in Division Two
    C. 8th in Division Two

23. In which season did Oxford achieve their highest ever position?
    A. 1980/81
    B. 1985/86
    C. 1986/87

24. How many times has Oxford United won league titles in total?
    A. 2
    B. 3
    C. 4

25. Which of these is a Oxford United supporters website?
    A. Raging Bull
    B. We all live in a Martin Keown house
    C. Yellow Army

26.   Who has made the most substitute appearances for the club?
    A. Graham Atkinson
    B. Joey Beauchamp
    C. Les Robinson

27.   What is the record transfer fee paid?
    A. £370,000
    B. £470,000
    C. £570,000

28.   Who was the record transfer fee paid for?
    A. Dean Saunders
    B. Dean Walling
    C. Dean Windass

29.   What is the record transfer fee received?
    A. £1.8 million
    B. £2.3 million
    C. £3 million

30.   Who was the record transfer fee received for?
    A. Michael Duberry
    B. Dave Kitson
    C. Kemar Roofe

Here are the answers to this block of questions.

A21. Oxford United have appeared in the top tier of English football, what used to be called the First Division, for three consecutive seasons.

A22. The highest the club has ever finished in the League is 18th in the top tier of English football (the old First Division).

A23. The club finished 18th in the First Division in both the 1985/86 and 1986/87 seasons. Unfortunately the following season the club finished bottom of the League and were relegated.

A24. Oxford United played four seasons in the Conference before being automatically promoted back to the Football League at the end of the 2009/10 season. Those were dark days.

A24. Oxford United were Second Division champions in 1984/85 and Third Division champions in 1967/68 and 1983/84.

A25. Yellow Army at yellowarmy.co.uk is a fans' website. Amongst its aims are to raise money for the Oxford United Youth and Community Trust. Raging Bull was a fabulous Oxford United fanzine from the 1990s.

A26. The club's super-sub is Joey Beauchamp. In his time at the club, he started 325 games and came off the bench 52 times too.

A27. The record transfer fee paid out by the club is £470,000.

A28. The club paid £470,000 to Aberdeen for Dean Windass in August 1998.

A29. The record transfer fee received by the club is £3 million.

A30. After protracted negotiations Oxford United received £3 million from Leeds United for Kemar Roofe in July 2016.

I hope you're having fun, and getting most of the answers right.

31. When did the club win the League Cup?
    A. 1974
    B. 1975
    C. 1976

32. What was the trophy also known as?
    A. The Barclays Cup
    B. The Littlewoods Cup
    C. The Milk Cup

33. Who did they beat in the final?
    A. Chelsea
    B. Fulham
    C. QPR

34. What was the score?
    A. 2-0
    B. 3-1
    C. 3-0

35. Who scored the first goal?
    A. Jeremy Charles
    B. Trevor Hebberd
    C. Ray Houghton

36. Who did they beat in the semi-final to reach Wembley?
    A. Aston Villa
    B. Norwich City
    C. Portsmouth

37. Who was the captain who lifted the Cup?
   A. Kevin Brock
   B. Dave Langan
   C. Malcolm Shotton

38. Who was the manager that day?
   A. Maurice Evans
   B. Brian Horton
   C. Jim Smith

39. How many Englishmen started the match for Oxford?
   A. 5
   B. 6
   C. 7

40. The manager gave his medal away to whom?
   A. Aaron Fish
   B. Ken Fish
   C. Michael Fish

Here are the answers to this block of questions.

A31. The club won its one and only major trophy in 1986.

A32. The League Cup was known as the Milk Cup, as it was sponsored by the Milk Marketing Board.

A33. They beat Queens Park Rangers in the final at Wembley Stadium on 20th April 1986.

A34. The score in the final was 3-0, and the game was really as one-sided as the score-line.

A35. Trevor Hebberd opened the scoring in the first half. Ray Houghton and Jeremy Charles scored the other goals in the second half.

A36. The semi-finals in the League Cup are two-legged affairs. Oxford beat Aston Villa 4-3 on aggregate. After drawing 2-2 away at Villa Park, Oxford won the second leg 2-1 at home.

A37. Malcolm Shotton was the captain on that glorious Spring day.

A38. Maurice Evans was the successful Oxford manager that season.

A39. Of the eleven players who started, seven were English. How times have changed.

A40. Evans gave away his winners medal to Ken Fish, the 72 year old physio/trainer, who had been at the club for 22 years, with Evans saying that Ken Fish deserved the medal more than he did.

Here is the next set of questions.

41. How many players have won full international caps whilst on the books at Oxford United?
   A. 6
   B. 10
   C. 14

42. Who was the first Oxford United player to win an international cap?
   A. John Aldridge
   B. Ray Houghton
   C. David Sloan

43. Which player won the most international caps whilst playing for Oxford?
   A. Dave Langan
   B. Jim Magilton
   C. Mark Watson

44. Which player has won the most international caps (including time at other clubs)?
   A. Ray Houghton
   B. Dean Saunders
   C. Mark Watson

45. How many goalkeepers have played for their country whilst at Oxford?
   A. 1
   B. 2

C. 3

46.   In 1998 Kevin Francis won two caps for
   which country?
   A. Antigua
   B. St Kitts and Nevis
   C. Trinidad and Tobago

47.   Who is the youngest player ever to
   represent the club?
   A. Jason Bateman
   B. Jason Priestley
   C. Jason Seacole

48.   Who is the youngest ever goal scorer
   for Oxford United?
   A. Andy Hutchinson
   B. Paul Moody
   C. Jason Seacole

49.   Who is the oldest player ever to
   represent the club?
   A. Alan Budge
   B. Alan Fudge
   C. Alan Judge

50.   How old was he at the time?
   A. 42 years and 124 days
   B. 43 years and 132 days
   C. 44 years and 176 days

Here are the answers to the last block of questions.

A41. A total of fourteen players have won full international caps whilst on the books at Oxford United.

A42. The first Oxford United player to get capped by his country was David Sloan who played twice for Northern Ireland in 1968.

A43. Jim Magilton won 18 caps for Northern Ireland whilst on the books at Oxford.

A44. Ray Houghton won 73 caps for Northern Ireland, from 1968 to 1997. Dean Saunders won 75 caps for Wales from 1986 to 2001. Mark Watson won 78 caps for Canada, from 1991 to 2004.

A45. Three goalkeepers have played for their countries whilst playing for Oxford. They are Andre Arendse for South Africa; Mick Kearns for Ireland and Paul Kee for Northern Ireland.

A46. Tall striker Francis won two caps for St Kitts and Nevis in 1998.

A47. Jason Seacole made his first team debut aged just 16 years and 149 days old against Mansfield Town on 7th September 1976. He went on to make 120 appearances fro the club.

A48. Jason Seacole is also down in the records as the club's youngest ever goal scorer. He scored 22 goals in his 120 appearances for the club.

A49. Alan Judge is the club's oldest ever outfield player.

A50. Alan Judge was 44 years and 176 days old when he played against Southend United on 6th November 2004. This is a record that is unlikely to ever be broken.

I hope you're learning some new facts about the club. Here we go with the next set of questions.

51. Oxford were relegated to the Conference in 2005/06. How many seasons did they play in the Conference before getting promoted?
   A. 2
   B. 3
   C. 4

52. In 1983, the then chairman Robert Maxwell wanted to merge Oxford with which club?
   A. Abingdon Town
   B. Reading
   C. Wycombe Wanderers

53. What was the name Maxwell suggested for the new merged club?
   A. Thames Valley Rovers
   B. Thames Valley Royals
   C. Thames Valley Wanderers

54. How many times have Oxford United reached the quarter finals of the FA Cup?
   A. 0
   B. 1
   C. 2

55. Which ex-manager went on to manage Aston Villa, Birmingham City and West Bromwich Albion?
   A. Ian Greaves

B. Ron Saunders

C. Jim Smith

56.   The car park at the ground is shared with what?
   A. A dry ski slope
   B. A cinema
   C. An ice rink

57.   When did ex-chairman Firoz Kassam buy the club?
   A. 1997
   B. 1998
   C. 1999

58.   What was the old ground called?
   A. The County Ground
   B. The Manor Ground
   C. The Radcliffe Ground

59.   Who were Oxford's opponents in the first game at the Kassam stadium?
   A. Chelsea
   B. Cheltenham Town
   C. Crystal Palace

60.   Who was the club's first non British or Irish manager?
   A. Ramon Diaz
   B. Juande Ramos
   C. Josef Venglos

Here are the answers to this block of questions.

A51. Oxford were cast adrift in the Conference for four long seasons from 2006/07 to 2009/10.

A52. In April 1983, Maxwell proposed merging United with Reading.

A53. Maxwell's, ahem, dream team was going to be called the Thames Valley Royals.

A54. Oxford United have reached the last eight of the FA Cup once, in the 1963/64 season.

A55. Ron Saunders was in charge at Oxford for just twelve games in 1969. He later went on to manage rivals Aston Villa, Birmingham City and West Bromwich Albion.

A56. Next to the ground is a multi-screen cinema, which often makes car parking spaces at the stadium limited.

A57. Firoz Kassam bought the club in April 1999.

A58. Prior to the Kassam Stadium, Oxford played its home games for many years at The Manor Ground.

A59. The first game staged at the Kassam Stadium was a friendly match against Crystal Palace on 4th August 2001.

A60. Argentine Ramon Diaz managed the club for 25 games from December 2004 to May 2005.

Let's give you some easier questions.

61. What is the traditional colour of the home shirt?
    A. Blue
    B. Green
    C. Yellow

62. What is the traditional colour of the away shirt?
    A. Black
    B. Grey
    C. White

63. What animal is on the club crest?
    A. A Bat
    B. An Ox
    C. A Phoenix

64. What is the name of Oxford United's match day programme?
    A. Oxford United FC Match Day Programme
    B. Oxford United Magazine
    C. Oxford United View

65. Who is considered as Oxford United's main rivals?
    A. Luton Town
    B. Swindon Town
    C. Wycombe Wanderers

66. Who is the current club sponsor?

A. Buildbase
B. Liontrust
C. Singha Beer

67. Who was the first club sponsor?
   A. BP
   B. BPCC
   C. BRC

68. Which of these have once sponsored the club?
   A. Database
   B. Homebase
   C. Buildbase

69. Who is currently the club chairman?
   A. Tiger Thanakarnjanasuth
   B. Darryl Eales
   C. Kelvin Thomas

70. In the last five league games against Swindon, how many have Swindon won?
   A. 0
   B. 1
   C. 2

Here are the answers to this block of questions.

A61. The colour most associated with Oxford United for its home shirts is yellow.

A62. Oxford United's away kit colour has been a right mixture over the years, including white, red, red and black stripes, black and grey and in a number of shades too, but historically it has to be white that has been used most as the first choice away kit colour.

A63. An ox is on the club crest. The ox is above a representation of a ford (a small stream) to symbolise its location - Oxford.

A64. The catchy name of the match day programme is the Oxford United FC Match Day Programme.

A65. Although Wycombe and Luton can be considered rivals, Oxford United's main rivals are without doubt Swindon Town. It's a rivalry which attracts the biggest crowds and the one the fans care most about.

A66. Singha Beer, as brewed in Thailand, is the current club sponsor.

A67. The first season sponsors appeared on the club shirts was in 1982/83. This is when Robert Maxwell used the Oxford shirts to advertise his publishing empire BPCC (British Printing and Communication Corporation).

A68. Buildbase sponsored the club for ten seasons from 2001/02 to 2009/10.

A69. Sumrith "Tiger" Thanakarnjanasuth is the current club chairman.

A70. Swindon have not won a league game against Oxford in a very long time. The last time Swindon beat Oxford over 90 minutes was back in March 2001.

I hope you are enjoying this book. Here are some questions about the ground.

71. What is the stadium's capacity?
    A. 12,100
    B. 12,300
    C. 12,500

72. What is the name of the road the ground is on?
    A. Grenada Avenue
    B. Greenfly Drive
    C. Grenoble Road

73. Which stand has the biggest capacity?
    A. The East Stand
    B. The North Stand
    C. The South Stand

74. What is considered the "main stand"?
    A. The East Stand
    B. The North Stand
    C. The South Stand

75. What is the club's record attendance ever?
    A. 21,106
    B. 22,136
    C. 23,196

76. What is the club's record attendance at the current ground?
    A. 12,243

B. 12,324
C. 12,432

77. What is the club's record Football Conference attendance?
   A. 9,963
   B. 10,963
   C. 11,963

78. What is the size of the pitch?
   A. 110 x 70 yards
   B. 112 x 78 yards
   C. 115 x 75 yards

79. What is the postcode of the ground?
   A. OX2
   B. OX4
   C. OX5

80. Who performed at the ground in July 2006?
   A. Elton John
   B. Rod Stewart
   C. Take That

Here are the answers to this block of questions.

A71. The current stadium capacity is 12,500. Not bad for a ground with just three stands.

A72. The stadium is located on Grenoble Road.

A73. The North Stand has the largest capacity in the ground and is able to seat approximately 5,026 people.

A74. The South Stand is the main structure of the stadium, housing the changing rooms, the club offices, 28 glass fronted executive boxes, and a conference centre.

A75. The club's record attendance ever was 22,730 for the visit of Preston North End in and FA Cup 6th round tie on 29th February 1964.

A76. The record attendance at the Kassam is 12,243 on 6th May 2006. This was for Oxford's final match of the League Two season, where a 3-2 defeat by Leyton Orient sealed their relegation from the Football League.

A77. The record attendance ever for a non league match was 11,963 for play off second leg against Rushden and Diamonds on 3rd May 2010.

A78. The size of the pitch at the Kassam is 112 yards long by 78 yards wide. By way of comparison, Wembley's pitch is 115 yards long by 75 yards wide.

A79. The full postcode of the ground is OX4 4XP.

A80. On Monday 24th July 2006, as part of his "Red Piano" tour, Elton John performed in front of a sell out crowd of 17,500 fans at the Kassam Stadium.

Here is the next set of questions.

81.　　When did the club move to the Kassam?
A. 1999
B. 2000
C. 2001

82.　　Who was the club's first million pound sale?
A. Joey Beauchamp
B. Matt Elliott
C. Dean Saunders

83.　　What nationality is Cameron Brannagan?
A. English
B. Irish
C. Scottish

84.　　What is the club's official website address?
A. oufc.co.uk
B. oxford.com
C. oxfordunited.com

85.　　What is the club's official twitter account?
A. @OUFC
B. @OUFCOfficial
C. @OxfordUnited

86.   Which of these ex Chelsea players has been a loyal servant at the club?
   A. Peter Houseman
   B. Peter Osgood
   C. Peter Rhoades-Brown

87.   Which of these goalkeepers once played for the club?
   A. Jim Barron
   B. Peter Bonetti
   C. John Burridge

88.   When did the club turn professional?
   A. 1949
   B. 1952
   C. 1955

89.   How many spells did Jim Smith have as manager?
   A. 2
   B. 3
   C. 4

90.   When did the club leave the Southern League and get elected to the Fourth Division?
   A. 1960
   B. 1962
   C. 1964

Here are the answers to this set of questions.

A81. The club moved to the Kassam in 2001.

A82. Dean Saunders was the club's first million pound sale, being transferred to Derby County for exactly £1 million in October 1988.

A83. Brannagan was born in Manchester.

A84. The official website that details all the latest news for fans throughout the world is at www.oufc.co.uk

A84. @OUFCOfficial Is the official twitter account. It tweets multiple times daily and deserves far more followers than it has.

A86. Peter Rhoades-Brown has performed many vital behind the scenes roles at the club over the years, and is currently the Business Development Manager.

A87. Jim Barron appeared in goal 165 times between 1966 and 1970.

A88. The club turned professional in 1949.

A89.Jim Smith had three spells as manager. He started his first spell in 1981 which was without doubt his most successful as he led the club into the top tier of English football after consecutive promotions as champions in 1984 and 1985.

A90. After winning the Southern League for the second successive season, the club was elected to the Football League Division Four in 1962.

Let's wind up with the final set of questions.

91. In 1998, what was a fans' pressure group called?
    A. Foul
    B. Offside
    C. Substituted

92. Who started the 2019/20 season as manager?
    A. Pep Clotet
    B. Kane Fazackerley
    C. Karl Robinson

93. What position did Oxford finish at the end of the 2018/19 season?
    A. 12th
    B. 14th
    C. 16th

94. Who is the kit supplier as shown on the shirt?
    A. Puma
    B. Reebok
    C. Starter

95. How much did Kassam sell the club for in March 2006?
    A. £1.2 million
    B. £2 million
    C. £3.2 million

96. Who was the first Oxford United manager after the cub turned professional in 1949?
   A. Gerry Summers
   B. Harry Thompson
   C. Arthur Turner

97. What is now on the site of the Manor Ground?
   A. A hospital
   B. An ice rink
   C. A sports centre

98. Which of these sports have been played at the Kassam?
   A. Rugby 7s
   B. Rugby League
   C. Rugby Union

99. Who is Oxford United's longest serving manager of all time?
   A. Jim Smith
   B. Arthur Turner
   C. Chris Wilder

100. Which of these "celebrities" support the club?
   A. Richard Branson
   B. Tim Henman
   C. Timmy Mallett

101. What is the statue located outside the ground?

A. A bear
B. A carthorse
C. An ox

Here are the answers to the last set of questions.

A91. During 1998, with the club in dire financial straits, a group of fans set up a pressure group called Fighting for Oxford United's Life (FOUL).

A92. Karl Robinson started the 2019/20 season as manager / head coach having been appointed on 22nd March 2018.

A93. Oxford United finished the 2018/19 season in a respectable 12th place.

A94. Puma are the official kit supplier.

A95. Kassam sold the club for approximately £2 million to Nick Merry on 21st March 2006. Kassam still owns the ground and associated land though, which is valued anywhere from £12-20 million.

A96. Oxford United's first manager after the club turned professional in 1949 was Harry Thompson. He was in charge from July 1949 until November 1958, overseeing 466 matches.

A97. The site of the old Manor Ground was sold for £12 million and the stadium was later demolished. The land is now occupied by a private hospital.

A98. Rugby Union side London Welsh used the stadium as their home ground for three seasons from 2012/13 to 2014/15.

A99. Arthur Turner managed the club from 1959 to 1969 being in charge of 504 games in total and is thus our longest serving manager of all time. He led the club to promotion from the old Southern League into the Football League, and was also in charge as Oxford won promotion from the Fourth Division in 1965 and won the Third Division in 1968.

A100. Branson, Henman and Mallett are all supporters of the club. Give yourself a bonus point if you knew that.

A101. A stunning bronze statue of an ox stands outside the stadium. It was unveiled in 2008, and is popular amongst fans.

That's a great question to finish with. That's it. I hope you enjoyed this book, and I hope you got most of the answers right.

I also hope you learnt one or two new things about the club and if you saw anything wrong, please contact us via the glowwormpress.com website.

If you did enjoy the book, please show your support and leave a positive review on Amazon.

Come on you Yellows.

Printed by Amazon Italia Logistica S.r.l.
Torrazza Piemonte (TO), Italy